MARRIAGE LEASE
A New Concept

FANY ROJAS

Contents

Acknowledgment

I have to start by thanking my good friend Michael Holton for being the brains behind the marriage lease concept. He not only sparked this idea but also trusted me to pen down this book. Together, we both stand firm in the belief that tying the knot later in life can bring about its own set of challenges. So, why not introduce a fresh approach to marriage like a lease that can be renewed or extended, without the heartache of a messy divorce?

My heartfelt gratitude goes out to my children, the pillars of my strength and inspiration. Kyle and Claire, your unwavering love and support fuel me every day. I am also deeply thankful to my dear friend Sofia Brandon for working with me to bring these pages to life.

Introduction

Marriage Lease: A New Concept

In a world where love is often portrayed as a feeling that should last a lifetime, the reality is that love is a verb, an action that requires continuous effort and dedication. The traditional notion of marriage, with its "till death do us part" commitment, doesn't offer a framework that helps partners get their needs met. When our needs are met the fire of love can burn brightly making better odds for a lasting partnership.

In the journey of life, our paths often lead us to unexpected crossroads, where the complexities of relationships and the intricacies of commitment take center stage. For those embarking on a second union later in life, the traditional landscape of marriage and partnership may not fully encapsulate the nuanced experiences and aspirations that define their path together.

In these pages we will challenge the conventional wisdom surrounding marriage and relationships. We propose a paradigm shift that acknowledges the dynamic nature of love and the importance of actively nurturing it.

Just as a traditional lease agreement allows for the renewal of terms and conditions, we believe that a similar approach to marriage can provide the necessary motivation to invest in the ongoing cultivation of love.

This book takes the marriage contract into a more elastic space where it functions like a lease with defined terms and opportunities for renewal. This shift in function encourages couples to proactively maintain the vitality of their relationship.

With thought-provoking insights and practical guidance, we invite you to consider the potential benefits of a model that aligns more closely with the evolving needs and aspirations of modern couples.

Looking together into this non-traditional approach to commitment, we hope to inspire meaningful conversations and reflections that will resonate with couples embarking on the unique journey of a second union.

As we explore this new concept, we encourage you to open to the possibilities it presents for renewing commitment, fostering open communication, and redefining the landscape of partnership in ways that honor the experiences, aspirations, and complexities of later-life relationships.

Join us as we challenge the status quo and empower people to own their love story!

Chapter 1

Understanding Marriage Leases

At the heart of every relationship lies a commitment—a promise to journey through life together, facing its joys and challenges as a united front. For many, this commitment is formalized through the institution of marriage, a timeless tradition that has symbolized love, unity, and partnership across cultures and generations.

However, as our lives evolve and our experiences shape our perspectives, the concept of commitment in relationships has itself undergone transformation, giving rise to alternative approaches that offer flexibility, reflection, and renewal.

For couples entering second unions later in life, particularly those with no desire for children together, the idea of a marriage lease presents an alternative approach to fostering lasting, meaningful, and flexible partnerships.

Exploring the Concept of Marriage Leases

The concept of a marriage lease introduces a paradigm shift in the traditional understanding of commitment and partnership. Rather than a lifetime vow, a marriage lease offers the opportunity to revisit and potentially renew the commitment to the relationship on a regular basis, typically once a year.

This approach acknowledges the dynamic nature of relationships and provides a framework for ongoing reflection and renegotiation of the terms of commitment.

Historical and Cultural Perspectives

Let's take a trip back in time to explore the history and culture of marriage in North America dating back to the early colonial period in the 1600s and 1700s. Back in those days, marriage was seen as a blend of legal and religious practices that focused on the importance of having children and building strong family units. However, as time went on, the concept of marriage evolved due to various cultural, social, and legal changes.

During the early colonial era marriage was all about ensuring economic and social stability for families. Marriages were often arranged based on factors like social status, wealth, and family ties. These unions weren't just about love; they helped families do things like expand land ownership and establish political connections.

In this period marriage was heavily regulated by the church and was seen as a sacred religious ceremony. Divorce was not allowed. Society expected couples to stay together for life. Having sex before marriage or an adulterous affair was asking for serious trouble with both the church and the law.

Moving into the 19th century, marriage began to take on a more romantic and companionate vibe. The rise of the middle class and the Industrial Revolution led to a change in the way people viewed tying the knot. Matrimony was starting to shape into more than a means of family economics.

As marriage became more about love and romance in modern times, it might have contributed to the rising divorce rates we see in the statistics from the 1980s onward. The change from practical views of marriage in the 19th century to a focus on emotions and connection in later years could have impacted how relationships work and why some marriages don't last. Societal norms shifted as well and it became more acceptable for people to divorce.

According to the American Psychological Association, since the 1980's around 50% of marriages in the United States end in divorce.

Other statistics on divorce in America include:

- The average age for couples getting divorced is 30 years old.
- The average length of a marriage ending in divorce is 8 years.
- The divorce rate is higher for second and third marriages compared to first marriages.
- Women are more likely to initiate divorce proceedings, with 69% of divorces being initiated by women.
- The most common reason for divorce is communication problems, followed by infidelity and financial issues.
- The divorce rate is higher among couples with lower levels of education and income.
- The state with the highest divorce rate is Nevada, with a rate of 4.4 divorces per 1,000 people.
- The state with the lowest divorce rate is Hawaii, with a rate of 1.8 divorces per 1,000 people.
- The divorce rate has been declining among younger couples but increasing among older couples.
- Children of divorced parents are more likely to experience emotional and behavioral problems.

So, can anything be done to help the seeming mad rush to un-tie the knot? There are likely a million things. But for the purpose of this text, we are going to focus on one. The one nestled in the middle of the statistics list that says communication problems cause divorce more than any other thing, even infidelity and financial woes. Who knows, if communication were better might couples be able to work through affairs and money matters a little better? I like to think so. And a marriage lease can be a great way to start.

Throughout history, the institution of marriage has been deeply intertwined with cultural, religious, and legal norms, often carrying with it a sense of permanence and lifelong obligation. This new concept of marriage leases challenges these long-standing traditions, prompting a re-examination of the societal and cultural expectations surrounding commitment and partnership.

Comparing Marriage Leases to Traditional Legal Marriage

A traditional legal marriage comes with a binding contract intended to stand the test of time yet offers a couple vague directives that tell them little about how to stay together. Instructions like "in sickness and in health" and "till death do us part" are often piled on to expectations set by Hollywood movies, and ideas from friends and family that leave couples with no real clarity about how to stay together.

A marriage lease can take some of the guesswork and hoping for the best out of the relationship equation. By clearly establishing the terms of the relationship upfront and then revisiting them at regular intervals, a marriage lease invites the couple to share and reflect on their experiences, aspirations, and evolving needs.

The most important conditions of their partnership get brought out into the open, clarified, and modified if needed allowing couples to design their partnership to align with what is important to them at any point in time.

Unlike traditional legal marriage, where you sign a contract meant to last forever, a marriage lease offers a more flexible and adjustable approach to commitment. By checking in on the relationship terms regularly, a marriage lease gives the couple the chance to rethink and discuss the conditions of their partnership, allowing them to consider their experiences, dreams, and changing needs within the context of their relationship.

Why do couples who have been together for a long time, decide to get married, and then later separate? What are the contributing factors to this phenomenon?

It's not uncommon for long-term partners to decide to get married after being together for years, only to quickly opt for a divorce. What could be causing this phenomenon? While we can never pinpoint the exact reasons why specific couples choose to end their relationships, I have a theory about this trend...

Each of us holds expectations about what marriage will bring to our relationship, for better or for worse. Some may expect that nothing will change except for wearing rings and throwing a big party, while others anticipate a complete transformation where their relationship reaches a new level, altering how they have engaged with the world so far.

Neither of these assumptions is incorrect. However, the problem occurs when the two individuals getting married fail to communicate their expectations. One partner anticipates, for example, that the marriage will enhance their intimate life, leading to more adventurous experiences due to increased trust. Meanwhile, the other partner envisions the marriage as an opportunity to travel together and never have to journey alone again.

Issues arise when these expectations remain unspoken. After the wedding, one partner may be disappointed, thinking, "Why was our honeymoon so uneventful? Where is the excitement I anticipated?"

Simultaneously, the other partner might wonder, "Why don't they want to explore a new city with me next weekend? I thought we would be inseparable now!" Do you now see the dilemma that can arise from this lack of communication?

Clearly, if it were that straightforward, finding a solution would be a breeze: have a conversation with your partner regarding your marriage expectations! This initial dialogue is crucial. However, let's face it: a significant portion of the time, many of us are unaware of our own expectations. Quantifying and expressing these desires is challenging. Defining what marriage signifies to you can be elusive.

It's likely that your views on marriage are influenced by or in response to the relationships you were exposed to while growing up. Discussing your parents' marriages or relationships can be beneficial in understanding these influences. Exploring the dynamics of other people's relationships can also help you clarify your own values.

Is marriage primarily about constant togetherness, supporting each other's individual pursuits without insecurity, engaging in adventurous intimacy, or enjoying cozy moments on the couch? Is it about establishing a shared home or traveling the world as a pair? Does it involve feeling secure enough in your commitment to navigate long-distance work opportunities on opposite sides of the country?

In both marriage and wedding planning, it is crucial to stay alert and conscious of the expectations and roles you and your partner are assuming. For unconventional heterosexual couples, the most common source of trouble often stems from societal norms dictating traditional gender roles and family dynamics. These ingrained assumptions can lead to situations where partners unwittingly slip into stereotypical husband and wife roles without even recognizing it. It is essential for couples to remain vigilant and actively challenge these norms to ensure they are living their own authentic lives together.

It is often bewildering to witness couples who have enjoyed years of happiness as partners suddenly struggle once they become spouses. This change may indicate that they held divergent expectations regarding the institution of marriage within their relationship. Perhaps they neglected to communicate these expectations or found it challenging to express their differences.

The lesson here? Communication is key. If you uncover significant disparities, it might be beneficial to seek premarital counseling. Strive to understand not only your own values but also those of your partner. While it would be wonderful if your values aligned perfectly, reality often requires compromise. This is where a marriage lease can be helpful. Even if you decide to marry again, it will make you accountable and help manage individual expectations.

Chapter 2

Navigating Relationships in Later Life

As we journey through life's different stages, our relationships and how they work can go through some pretty big shifts. When we reach later life, dealing with relationships can bring its own set of challenges and chances, like second marriages, blended families, differing views on having kids, and the quest for emotional happiness and personal development. In this chapter, we'll dig deeper into these different aspects and share some tips on how couples can handle the twists and turns of relationships keeping a love connection as they get older.

Unique Dynamics of Second Marriages

Tying the knot for the second time later in life brings a mix of unique dynamics and factors into play. Unlike first marriages, second time around unions can involve people with decades of life experiences, set ways of doing things, and often children from previous relationships. Dealing with so many moving parts calls for a lot of talking, give-and-take, and empathy from both partners. We'll dive into the ups and downs of second marriages, sharing tips on how to lay the groundwork for a strong and lasting partnership in your later years.

Addressing the Challenges of Blended Families

Dealing with blended families, where kids from past relationships come together in a new family setup, can be complex. Couples might need to figure out how to handle the intricacies of co-parenting by setting up clear rules and promoting togetherness and empathy among all family members. Here are some pointers on how to tackle these challenges:

1   Keep the Lines of Communication Open: Make sure everyone feels comfortable sharing their thoughts and feelings. Regular family meetings can help address issues and come up with solutions together.

2   Set Clear Expectations: Define roles, rules, and routines within the family to provide structure and stability. Consistency is key to making sure everyone feels secure.

3   Respect Everyone's Differences: Embrace the unique backgrounds and personalities of each family member. Encourage understanding and acceptance of each other's quirks. Celebrate diversity and promote inclusivity.

4   Strengthen Family Bonds: Plan activities that bring the family together and create shared memories. Spending quality time as a family can help build strong relationships.

5   Work Together with Co-Parents: Collaborate with ex-partners or co-parents to ensure a united front when it comes to parenting. Maintain open communication and prioritize the well-being of the children.

6   Consider Professional Help: Seeking guidance from a family therapist or counselor can provide valuable tools and insights to improve family dynamics and address challenges.

7   Be Patient and Flexible: Blending families takes time and patience. Stay flexible and understanding as everyone adjusts to the new family dynamic. Give yourself and others the time needed to adapt.

8   Celebrate Successes: Acknowledge and celebrate achievements and positive moments within the blended

family. Recognize efforts to strengthen relationships and create a harmonious environment.

Being supportive and inclusive of one another helps us work through challenges and build strong, loving relationships that are good for everyone in the family.

Considerations for Couples with No Desire for Children

Some couples early or later in life may realize they have no desire to have children. This decision can bring about its own set of considerations and societal pressures. We will look into the various factors that couples may want to consider when making this choice.

1. Personal Values and Goals: Make sure you both agree on not having kids and think about what you want from life together without them.
2. Money Matters: Consider how not having kids can affect your finances. You might have more freedom to focus on your careers, save for the future, and do things you enjoy.
3. Lifestyle Choices: Think about how your decision will impact your lifestyle - like travel, hobbies, and taking care of yourselves. Without kids, you may have more time for these things.
4. Support System: Plan for support as you get older since you won't have children to rely on. Build a network of friends and family who can help out when needed.
5. Relationship Dynamics: Discuss how not having kids might change your relationship in the long run. Find ways to stay connected and happy without the experience of parenting.

Insights and Tips:

- Be Open with Each Other: Talk honestly about your choice not to have kids. Listen to each other and work together to shape your future without feeling pressured by others.
- Set Boundaries: People may question your decision, but it's important to stand by it. Set boundaries with others, communicate your choice clearly, and don't feel the need to justify it.
- Find Support: Look for groups or friends who understand and support your decision. Having a community that shares your views can make you feel less alone.
- Focus on Personal Growth: Invest in yourselves and your relationship. Pursue your interests, education, or career goals, and nurture your bond with each other.
- Create Meaningful Connections: Find purpose and fulfillment in your lives by giving back to your community, volunteering, or pursuing activities that bring you joy and a sense of contribution.

Emotional Well-Being and Personal Growth in Later Life Relationships

As people age, prioritizing emotional well-being and personal growth within their relationships becomes increasingly important.

Here are some ideas that may help couples maintain open communication, nurture their interests, and support each other's development.

1. Talk Things Out:

- Make sure to have regular, honest chats with your partner. Share your thoughts, feelings, and worries openly.
- Listen to each other and try to understand where the other is coming from.
- Deal with any disagreements calmly and respectfully.

2. Pursue Your Passions:

- Encourage each other to explore hobbies and interests that make you happy.
- Respect each other's need for alone time to do your own thing.
- Share your experiences and discoveries with each other to strengthen your bond.

3. Support Each Other's Goals:

- Be each other's cheerleader when it comes to personal growth and goals, whether it's learning something new or trying out different opportunities.
- Offer motivation, support, and positive feedback to help each other reach your personal milestones.
- Celebrate each other's wins and accomplishments to feel proud and connected.

4. Be Great Companions:

- Spend quality time doing things you both enjoy together.
- Create memories and shared experiences that bring you closer.
- Lean on each other for support, company, and comfort when times get tough.

5. Keep the Spark Alive:

- Foster intimacy through physical touch, emotional closeness, and shared moments.
- Keep your romantic relationship strong by showing love, affection, and gratitude.
- Talk openly about what you both want to maintain a deep connection and understanding.

6. Show Mutual Respect:

- Treat each other with kindness, respect, and thoughtfulness.
- Value each other's opinions, boundaries, and independence.
- Be patient, understanding, and willing to compromise in times of disagreement.

These steps can lead to a stronger bond, increased satisfaction, and a more fulfilling partnership as you both age together.

Chapter 3

Embracing Change and Flexibility in Relationships

In today's world where relationships are constantly changing and people value their independence, the idea of a marriage lease is gaining popularity as a modern take on commitment. This fresh concept blends the security of marriage with the flexibility of lease agreements, highlighting the importance of embracing change and staying adaptable for a strong partnership.

Renewal isn't just about paperwork—it's a meaningful way to show dedication and take stock of the relationship. Similar to renewing a lease or contract to keep things up-to-date and beneficial, couples can come together yearly to reaffirm their bond, reflect on their progress, and set new goals for the future. This practice fosters connection, encourages honest communication, and empowers partners to actively shape the path of their relationship.

Flexibility lies at the core of the marriage lease concept, allowing couples to navigate life's changes and challenges with grace and understanding. By acknowledging that people evolve over time, this approach empowers partners to adapt their relationship dynamics, expectations, and goals accordingly. Flexibility fosters resilience, empathy, and a deep sense of partnership, enabling couples to weather storms and celebrate victories together.

The Benefits of Revisiting Commitment Annually

Taking a yearly check-in on our commitments is like giving ourselves a chance to hit the reset button, reflect on how far we've come, and get pumped up for what's next. It's a time to see if our goals are still on track, tweak them if needed, and show our dedication to making things happen.

When we make it a habit to revisit our commitments regularly, we keep them fresh and meaningful, even when life throws us a curveball. It's a way to pat ourselves on the back for what we've achieved, spot areas where we can do better, and set new targets for the coming year. This annual ritual infuses our commitments with a new sense of purpose and energy, helping us stay motivated and focused on what truly matters to us.

So, by taking the time to review our commitments each year, we're not just staying on course—we're supercharging our dedication, fueling our enthusiasm, and setting ourselves up for success in the days and months ahead.

Fostering Open Communication and Reflection

When it comes to keeping our commitments fresh and flexible, open communication and reflection are like our trusty sidekicks. Creating a space where we can chat openly and honestly helps us share how we're feeling, what we're aiming for, and what's bugging us with our partners. These heart-to-heart talks give us a deeper understanding of where we're at in our commitments and help us figure out how we can grow and change together.

By having these real and caring conversations, we get to peek behind the curtain of our relationships and see what makes them tick. It's a chance for us to team up with our partners to find new ways to evolve and adapt to whatever life throws our way. And when we take a moment to look inward and reflect on our own motivations, values, and hurdles, we get a clearer picture of who we are and what we want, making us more aware and responsible in our commitments.

Addressing Emotional and Psychological Implications

Renewing our commitments and staying flexible isn't always easy- it can stir up a whole mix of emotions and thoughts. It's normal for couples to feel a bit vulnerable, nervous, or even a little resistant when facing changes in their commitments. Addressing the emotional and psychological implications of renewal is crucial for the well-being of both partners.

The key is to recognize and deal with these feelings in a caring and understanding way. Professional guidance and support may also be sought to navigate challenging emotions and promote personal growth.

When we acknowledge and address our partner's emotional and psychological responses with empathy and support, we're laying down a solid foundation for personal growth and resilience. By showing that we're there for each other through the ups and downs, we create a safe space where we can all grow stronger together and fortify our commitment along the way. After all, facing challenges and changes is part of the journey, and tackling them together can make our bond even more unbreakable.

Keeping things interesting and flexible is like giving our commitments a boost and helping them go the distance. When we're open to change, check in on our commitments each year, have honest chats, reflect on our feelings and thoughts, and deal with the emotional stuff, we're basically setting ourselves up for commitments that can stand the test of time.

Chapter 4

Navigating the Complexities of Marriage Leases

As we dig deeper into the details of marriage leases, it's essential to grasp the ins and outs of handling money and assets in this special setup. In this chapter, we will examine the potential benefits and drawbacks of marriage leases, the importance of seeking legal counsel and community support, and the complexities involved in addressing the dissolution of a marriage lease.

Managing Finances and Assets in a Marriage Lease

One of the fundamental aspects of a marriage lease is the management of finances and assets. In a traditional marriage, financial matters are often governed by established laws and customs. However, in the context of a marriage lease, partners have the opportunity to customize their financial arrangements to suit their individual needs and circumstances.

It is crucial for partners entering into a marriage lease to engage in open and honest discussions about their financial expectations and responsibilities. This may involve creating a detailed plan for managing joint expenses, individual assets, estate and retirement planning and potential investments. Additionally, partners should consider the implications of sharing debts and liabilities and the mechanisms for resolving financial disputes should they arise.

Potential Benefits and Drawbacks of Marriage Leases

Marriage leases offer a range of potential benefits, including flexibility in structuring financial arrangements, clarity in defining each partner's rights and obligations, and the ability to address specific concerns related to assets and inheritance. Moreover, a well-constructed marriage lease can provide a sense of security and stability for partners entering into a second union. However, it is important to acknowledge the potential drawbacks of marriage leases as well. Complexities may arise in managing joint finances, especially when partners have varying levels of financial independence or when they have children from previous relationships. Furthermore, the dissolution of a marriage lease can present unique challenges, as it involves navigating legal and financial matters within the context of a non-traditional marital arrangement.

Seeking Legal Counsel and Community Support

Given the intricate nature of marriage leases, seeking legal counsel is essential for couples navigating this terrain. Experienced legal professionals can provide valuable guidance in structuring the terms of the marriage lease, ensuring compliance with relevant laws, and addressing potential contingencies. In addition to legal support, community resources and support networks can play a pivotal role in assisting couples in second unions. Engaging with support groups, counseling services, and financial advisors can offer couples valuable insights and emotional support as they navigate the complexities of marriage leases.

For couples navigating the complexities of marriage leases, seeking legal counsel and community support is highly beneficial. Here are some types of support groups and counseling services that can be helpful in this context:

1 Support Groups for Couples: These support groups specifically cater to couples in second unions or dealing

with complex marital agreements. They provide a platform for sharing experiences, receiving advice, and gaining emotional support from people in similar situations.

2 Marriage Counseling Services: Professional marriage counselors can help couples work through issues related to their marriage lease. They can provide guidance on communication, conflict resolution, and decision-making, which are crucial in maintaining a healthy relationship within the framework of a marriage lease.

3 Financial Advisors: Given the financial implications of marriage leases, consulting with a financial advisor can help couples make informed decisions about their financial future. Financial advisors can provide guidance on budgeting, investments, and long-term financial planning tailored to the couple's specific situation.

4 Community-based Counseling Services: Many communities offer counseling services for couples facing challenges in their relationships. These services can provide a safe space for couples to discuss their concerns, explore solutions, and strengthen their bond within the context of a marriage lease.

5 Online Support Forums: Online forums and communities focused on relationships and marriage can also be valuable sources of support. Couples can anonymously seek advice, share their experiences, and connect with others facing similar challenges.

Addressing the Complexity of Ending a Marriage Lease

The decision to end a marriage lease is a multifaceted process that requires careful consideration and planning. Partners will want to address the division of assets, financial responsibilities, and potential support arrangements in the event of a dissolution. It is crucial for couples to outline clear procedures for terminating the marriage lease and to establish mechanisms for resolving disputes amicably. Furthermore, partners should be mindful of the emotional and psychological impact of ending a marriage lease, particularly if children are involved. Open communication and a commitment to mutual respect can facilitate a smoother transition during this challenging period.

To sum up, handling finances and assets in a marriage lease demands thoughtful preparation, transparent communication, and a deep comprehension of the legal and financial consequences.

Chapter 5

Building Trust and Intimacy

As we continue exploring this new concept of a marriage lease, building and maintaining trust and intimacy becomes paramount. In this chapter, we will look into the unique dynamics of non-traditional commitments and how to foster trust, establish clear boundaries, nurture emotional connections, and support each other's individual growth in the context of a renewed commitment.

Fostering Trust and Intimacy in Non-Traditional Commitment

Whether it's a second marriage, a blended family, or a long-term partnership after a previous relationship, trust and intimacy play a crucial role in the success of these unions.

Building trust in such relationships often requires a delicate balance of openness, honesty, and understanding. It involves respecting each other's past experiences while also creating a shared vision for the future. Intimacy, both emotional and physical, requires patience and communication as partners navigate their individual histories and come together to create a new bond.

Establishing Clear Boundaries and Expectations

In any relationship setting clear boundaries and expectations is essential for creating a sense of security and understanding. In the context of second unions, this becomes even more crucial as partners bring with them past experiences and possibly even children from previous relationships. Open and honest conversations about each other's needs, personal space, and responsibilities can lay the foundation for a healthy and respectful partnership.

Here are some examples of clear boundaries and expectations that can be established in a relationship:

1   Personal Space: Giving each other room to breathe and have some alone time or pursue individual interests without feeling crowded.
2   Communication: Being open and honest with each other, listening actively, and expressing thoughts and feelings respectfully.
3   Money Matters: Agreeing on who pays for what, setting up a budget, and discussing financial goals together to avoid conflicts over money.
4   Parenting: If there are kids from previous relationships, talking about parenting styles, discipline, and how involved each partner will be in the children's lives.
5   Household Chores: Dividing up household tasks and responsibilities to make sure both partners feel like they're doing their fair share.
6   Quality Time: Making a point to spend time together, plan dates, and nurture the relationship to keep the connection strong.
7   Dealing with Exes: Setting boundaries with ex-partners to ensure that past relationships don't interfere with the current one.
8   Emotional Support: Being there for each other during tough times, showing empathy, and communicating your needs for emotional support.

Nurturing Emotional Connection and Romance

In the midst of life's demands nurturing emotional connection and romance is vital for keeping the spark alive. Finding time for each other, engaging in meaningful conversations, and expressing appreciation for one another are essential components of maintaining a strong emotional bond.

Romance may take different forms in non-traditional commitments, but the underlying sentiment remains the same – to show love and appreciation for your partner. By prioritizing emotional connection and keeping the romance alive, couples can strengthen their bond and weather the inevitable challenges that arise.

Prioritizing emotional connection in a relationship means making a deliberate effort to nurture and strengthen the emotional bond between partners. This involves understanding each other's feelings, thoughts, and needs, and actively working to support and validate each other emotionally.

Here are some ways to prioritize emotional connection in a relationship:

1 Communication: Talking openly and honestly, listening attentively, and showing empathy towards your partner's feelings are essential for building emotional connection.

2 Quality time: Spending meaningful time together without distractions is important for emotional closeness. Whether it's engaging in activities together or having heartfelt conversations, quality time strengthens the emotional bond.

3 Support and validation: Being there for each other, offering understanding, and celebrating each other's victories are ways to nurture emotional connection and create a sense of mutual support.

4   Expressing appreciation: Regularly showing gratitude and acknowledging your partner's efforts helps reinforce emotional connection. Small acts of kindness and words of appreciation can make a big difference in strengthening the bond.

5   Showing affection: Physical touch, gestures of affection, and expressions of love play a significant role in fostering emotional intimacy. These actions help reinforce feelings of closeness and connection.

6   Building trust: Trust is a cornerstone of emotional connection. Being honest, dependable, and trustworthy in your relationship helps create a strong emotional bond.

Developing trust and closeness in non-traditional relationships takes time, honest communication, and a real understanding of each other's needs. By actively focusing on emotional connection couples can deepen their understanding of each other, strengthen their bond, and create a supportive and lasting relationship.

Chapter 6

What About Sex?

Qualities of a Healthy Sexual Relationship

Variety is key, and even the happiest couples are not always perfectly in tune. Let's explore further insights from researchers on establishing a strong sexual foundation.

Even though more than 80% of individuals express satisfaction with their sex lives within the first six months of a relationship, a considerable proportion—43% of men and 55% of women—still report contentment years later, as outlined in a 2016 study published in the Journal of Sex Research by the Kinsey Institute at Indiana University. While the initial six months are typically the most passionate and intense, with these feelings diminishing over time, the research demonstrates that there are numerous ways to introduce novelty and reignite satisfaction. Here are six strategies that sexually fulfilled couples utilize to maintain a vibrant sexual relationship, often lasting for decades.

1. Sex is not a daily occurrence

Some days, after a tiring day of work and an evening spent with family, the last thing you may feel up to is engaging in intimate activities. The good news is that research shows it's not necessary to do so. A study that surveyed over 30,000 long-term monogamous couples discovered that while increased frequency of sexual activity was linked to greater reported happiness, this benefit plateaued at once a week. Couples who had sex four times a week reported similar levels of relationship satisfaction as those who engaged in sexual activities only once a week. Many couples may feel pressured to have sex frequently, leading to avoidance due to feeling overwhelmed. However, what truly matters is the quality of the sexual experiences rather than the quantity.

2. Intimacy thrives even during mundane moments

According to a 2016 University of Rochester study published in the Journal of Personality and Social Psychology, a couple's sexual desire for each other is positively correlated with their attentiveness to each other's emotional needs outside the bedroom. This finding challenges the conventional wisdom of the 'intimacy-desire paradox,' which suggests that increased closeness diminishes attraction by eliminating the sense of novelty and mystery. In a six-week diary study involving 100 long-term couples, those who perceived their partners as most responsive to their needs also reported the highest levels of libido.

Feeling valued fosters feelings of desirability, subsequently boosting one's own sexual drive.

3. The three magic words: "I love you"

The study mentioned that expressing love seems to be the go-to communication strategy for couples who are content.

A study from Chapman University in 2016, published in the Journal of Sex Research, found that about three-quarters of men and women in happy relationships say these words during their recent intimate moments. The study mentioned that expressing love seems to be the go-to communication strategy for couples who are content. Saying "I love you" during sex helps you connect with your partner on a deeper level, which is crucial for a fulfilling sex life. The research also revealed that one in three women and one in four men who are happy with their sex lives feel closer to their partner emotionally during sex compared to the early days of their relationship.

4. It's not just the same old routine

Breaking away from the usual routine is key to a fulfilling sex life After being together for an extended period, relationships can become somewhat predictable. Therefore, the more diverse sexual activities a couple explores, the greater their satisfaction. While many couples in the study mentioned reading sex advice materials, the truly satisfied couples were those who put the suggestions into practice. Trying new positions was the most popular choice, alongside activities such as enjoying a sensual bath together, exchanging massages, and openly discussing or acting out fantasies.

5. Date Nights: Simply Adult Play dates

It's possible that partners who engage in exciting and new activities together tend to have a stronger bond. A study in the Journal of Personality and Social Psychology suggests that couples who participate in thrilling activities are happier. For example, researchers once had couples navigate an obstacle course while strapped together with Velcro - not your typical Friday night activity, but it seems to have had some positive effects.

Engaging in playful activities may help prevent relationship boredom, which can be detrimental. It's also possible that these adventures trigger brain neurotransmitters associated with sexual arousal. You don't have to plan extreme activities like skydiving; simply revisiting enjoyable pastimes together, such as biking or trying out new restaurants, can reignite the passion in your relationship. As long as you're doing it together, any fun activity has the potential to strengthen your connection.

6. Occasionally, "yes" means "eh"

The reality is that couples are not always perfectly aligned: as per research, 80% of couples experience a difference in sexual desires over time, where one partner desires sex while the other does not. Individuals who are more motivated to fulfill their partner's sexual needs tend to experience higher levels of sexual and relationship satisfaction. Essentially, choosing to engage in intimacy even when you would rather rest can lead to positive outcomes. By focusing on the benefits, such as making your partner feel loved and desired, couples can derive pleasure from the experience as well. However, does this imply that you should always comply with your partner's requests for sex when you're not in the mood? Not necessarily. A crucial aspect of these shared relationships involves both partners being attuned to each other's needs. This includes being understanding when your partner is not feeling inclined towards intimacy.

Chapter 7

Community and Societal Considerations

Couples considering a marriage lease will want to think about how their choice could be influenced by their culture and the community they live in.

It helps to speak openly about the challenges they face, get help if needed from their community, and keep in mind throughout that a marriage lease can give as much control and choice to the partners as they choose.

Cultural and Societal Implications of Marriage Leases

In many cultures around the world, marriage is deeply intertwined with tradition, societal expectations, and religious beliefs. These beliefs and traditions will likely be tested by this new concept making it all the better to keep lines of communication open. Couples will want to have honest conversations with their families, communities, and religious groups. By involving the people closest to them in their family and community they can promote better understanding and acceptance of their special way of renewing commitment while respecting their cultural background.

Challenging Traditional Norms and Expectations

Deciding to go for a marriage lease often goes against the traditional norms and expectations linked with marriage. Society might have set ideas about the right way to "do" marriage, putting pressure and judgment on couples taking a different route. It's important for couples to stay strong and speak up about the worth and importance of their chosen path. This way they add to the ongoing discussion about how relationships and family setups are changing in our society.

Taking Control of Your Relationship

Deciding to solidify your commitment with a marriage lease puts you in the driver's seat when it comes to steering your relationship. This approach allows partners to openly communicate and redefine the dynamics of their partnership, with a focus on respect, consent, and individual fulfillment. By embracing personal freedom and empowerment, couples can cultivate a strong relationship grounded in shared values, open dialogue, and a solid sense of collaboration.

In essence, marriage leases can come with a mix of cultural and societal impacts. They're not for everyone, but for those who are not keen on the traditional route, this could be an interesting alternative to explore!

Maintaining a Strong Relationship in the Face of Modern Challenges

New Data Supports the Value of Staying Together.
After finishing work and returning home, people bring their social connections with them. The prevalence of social media has simplified the process of finding support and engaging in conversations outside of traditional circles. In addition, it has made finding a new romantic partner more convenient in case communication issues arise. A person's faithfulness is closely tied to the options available to them. Nowadays, individuals of both genders believe they have numerous alternatives. They can reconnect with past romantic interests or explore the vast array of potential partners in online dating platforms.

While divorce might be viewed as a setback, it is no longer accompanied by the same level of stigma or complexity. Since 2010, every state in the U.S. has permitted individuals to end their marriages without assigning blame, often without the need for the spouse's consent. Mediators are streamlining the divorce process, making it more affordable and less burdensome. Resources such as self-help books and websites are now dedicated to promoting the idea of a "good divorce," a concept that was once considered unthinkable.

Many researchers have pointed out that the concept of lifelong monogamy is not a natural behavior for humans. In fact, a relatively small percentage of animal species practice lifelong mating, such as certain types of birds or species that are not conventionally attractive, like the Malagasy giant rat. One theory suggests that humans have adopted monogamy as a way to promote social unity and reduce male rivalry within communities.

For instance, in some species of birds like albatrosses or swans, lifelong monogamy is observed as a way to ensure successful reproduction and care for offspring. Similarly, in some primate species like gibbons, monogamous relationships help establish strong family units that contribute to the survival and well-being of the group.

In human societies, monogamy may have evolved as a social construct to maintain stability, reduce conflicts over mating partners, and foster cooperation among community members. By promoting long-term pair bonding, societies can establish a sense of trust, shared responsibility, and mutual support among individuals, which can be beneficial for the overall cohesion and functioning of the group.

However, what occurs naturally does not always align with what is beneficial. Monogamy offers a practical advantage in terms of conserving energy: it spares humans the need to expend time and effort on perpetually seeking new partners or coping with betrayals from existing ones.

Individuals in happy relationships tend to experience better health and financial well-being. They are less prone to strokes, heart disease, or depression, exhibit improved stress responses, and tend to recover quicker from health issues. The ability to share wealth and expenses may enable access to higher-quality healthcare.

The intriguing aspect is that as couples spend more time together, the sense of kindness tends to re-emerge. Studies show that in later stages of life, relationships often mirror the dynamics of the courtship period.

Research indicates that individuals who are able to maintain a long-term commitment in a relationship may find it to be a rewarding endeavor. Studies show that people that are in monogamous relationships tend to enjoy better health, greater wealth, and more satisfying sex lives compared to their single counterparts, and are likely to experience greater happiness throughout their lives.

How is this for an insensitive?

Chapter 8

Navigating Challenges and Renewing Vows

As we've seen in previous chapters, non-traditional commitment offers a path to successful and fulfilling relationships, but not without challenges.

In this chapter, we will share the experiences of couples who have faced and overcome obstacles in their non-traditional commitments. We hope their personal stories will offer lessons and practical tips for anyone wanting to approach renewing their vows in a non-traditional way.

Brooklyn and Colin

Brooklyn is a close friend of mine who I've always admired for her sense of freedom and unconventional approach to life.

When I first met her, she was already involved with Colin, but I didn't realize the nature of their commitment until I began writing this book. I knew they weren't interested in marriage, but I was surprised to learn about their unique yearly arrangement, which they referred to as "the list."

Their relationship had a special quality to it - despite not following traditional norms, they always appeared happy and deeply in love, even after spending many years together.

Brooklyn and Colin were hanging out at their favorite coffee spot, sipping on lattes and sharing jokes as usual. They'd been together for eight years, but their relationship was far from conventional.

Instead of opting for a traditional marriage, they came up with something unique - a marriage list that both of them had to sign and agree on! What started as a quirky idea had evolved into something truly meaningful.

It all began during a casual conversation about marriage and commitment. Brooklyn, a free spirit who valued her independence above all else, wasn't interested in following the usual path. Colin, having experienced a tough divorce in the past, was wary of rushing into another marriage.

So, they came up with this cool idea - a yearly "marriage list". It was their way of showing their love without the complications of a traditional marriage.

Not many people knew about it, just a few close friends who sometimes raised their eyebrows at the unconventional setup. But Brooklyn and Colin didn't let that bother them. To them, it made sense. It was a symbol of their commitment to each other, a reminder that love doesn't have to fit a standard mold.

Sitting in the cozy coffee shop that day, they clinked their mugs together in a quiet celebration, thankful for the strong connection they had. The time for renewing the list was coming up, but neither of them had any doubts about signing on for another year. Love doesn't come with a way of doing things, and for Brooklyn and Colin, that was just the way they preferred it.

Every year, on the anniversary of signing their list, Brooklyn and Colin would sit down and have a serious chat, treating their list like a roadmap for their relationship. They'd discuss what was going well, what needed work, and any new things they wanted to add. It was like a relationship check-up, a chance to communicate, understand each other, and grow together.

One year, Colin had let things slide a bit. Thanks to a packed schedule and too much stress at work he had gained twenty pounds. Brooklyn, who valued staying in shape, wasn't too pleased. She gave it to Colin straight – the extra weight wasn't doing his physique any favors plus the work stress had made him edgy and distant, nearly impossible to connect with. He had to invest in some self care or the deal between them would be seriously compromised. It was a wake-up call for him. He hit the gym, improved his diet and had a conversation with his boss to keep his lady happy, yes, but ultimately to get back into balance with himself.

These annual reviews kept things exciting and fresh for Colin and Brooklyn. They could address issues directly, set new objectives, and motivate each other to improve. It was like a love workout, keeping their relationship strong and vibrant.

Let's Make It Official... Sort Of

As they reached their fourth year as a couple, Brooklyn and Colin felt a deep longing for something extra special. Even though they had moved away from the idea of a typical marriage, they still wanted to commemorate their love in a significant manner. That's when they decided on a spiritual wedding ceremony.

They chose a serene garden setting where their closest friends and family came together to celebrate their love. A dear friend officiated as they opened their hearts, shared genuine vows, and reveled in the beautiful journey they had embarked on together.

The spiritual wedding was pure magic for Brooklyn and Colin, a mix of emotions and wonder. It was a tribute to their love, their special connection, and the path they'd walked together. As they danced under the starlit sky, they knew their love was something extraordinary, something that would endure.

That's just how Brooklyn and Colin rolled - renewing their marriage list every year with smiles and love. Their soulful wedding had marked a new chapter in their love story, filled with warmth, growth, and the freedom to evolve together. They recognized that love was a fantastic, ever-evolving adventure, and they treasured every moment!

I love that this type of unconventional partnership exists far beyond my friendship circle as well. In Hollywood!

Hollywood Couples

Goldie Hawn and Kurt Russell have been in a long-term relationship since 1983, but they've never married. Their relationship is often cited as an example of a successful, non-conventional type of partnership in Hollywood.

Goldie Hawn and Kurt Russell first met while filming "The One and Only, Genuine, Original Family Band" in 1966, but they didn't begin their romantic relationship until they co-starred in the film, "Swing Shift" in 1983.

Since then, they have become one of Hollywood's most enduring couples. Their relationship is often characterized as non-conventional because they chose not to get married despite being together for decades. Both Hawn and Russell speak openly about why they never tied the knot. They say the commitment to each other doesn't require a marriage certificate, that their love and dedication to each other are what truly matter.

They also emphasize the importance of independence and personal growth within their partnership.

Despite not being legally married, Goldie Hawn and Kurt Russell raised a blended family together, with children from previous marriages as well as one child, Wyatt Russell, whom they had together. Their commitment to each other and their family is a defining aspect of their relationship. Hawn and Russell's enduring partnership and dedication to each other have made them an iconic couple in Hollywood, and their non-conventional approach to their relationship has been an inspiration to many who value love, commitment, and independence in their own lives.

Hawn and Russell are not alone among high profile Hollywood couples. Couples in Hollywood who chose not to marry and have built successful, enduring relationships. Some of these couples include:

1   Oprah Winfrey and Stedman Graham: Media mogul Oprah Winfrey and businessman Stedman Graham have been together since 1986. Despite being engaged at one point, they never married, choosing instead to focus on their individual careers and maintaining a committed partnership.
2   Susan Sarandon and Tim Robbins: Academy Award-winning actors Susan Sarandon and Tim Robbins were in a relationship for over twenty years before they split in 2009. They never married but shared a strong partnership and raised two sons together.
3   Marisa Tomei and Logan Marshall-Green: Actress Marisa Tomei and actor Logan Marshall-Green are in a long-term relationship. They remain private about their relationship, but the media have noted their decision to forgo marriage.

These couples, like Goldie Hawn and Kurt Russell, show us that committed and enduring partnerships can thrive without traditional marriage. Their examples illustrate love and dedication in many forms, and how each couple is free to define their relationship on their own terms.

My Story

My last relationship taught me a lot. I had fallen deeply in love and thought I had found my person for life. We'll call him Jeff for privacy. Sadly, trust became an issue. I began to feel insecure as though there wasn't enough of a love connection to carry on. Out of desperation and frustration, I ended the relationship and moved out. We had been living comfortably and, for the most part, happily together for over two years during Covid when he couldn't travel for work. It was when he started traveling again that things took a turn for the worse. He struggled with being loyal.

After I moved out, we somehow found the words to talk about what wasn't working between us and decided to give it another shot, but I laid down some rules.

Here is the actual list of rules I gave my ex:

"This is not indicative of what normal is, but based on your past behaviors, I have to set boundaries and rules in order to make this relationship work."

Boundaries & Rules

- Share location
- Call to check in when you are travelling
- No hookups - in-person or online
- We prioritize our kids first, then us
- You will not get random girls' phone numbers
- Do not stare at other women in front of me
- We discuss all the guys' trips before you plan them. Same for me
- We will share passwords to our phones
- No secret appts

- Anniversaries are important
- Be selective with friendships, keeping them age-appropriate
- I want to get married before September of 2022-Prenup – no problem - run off to Vegas

If we can abide and accept these rules we will have a great future - otherwise, we need to go our separate ways."

I was both surprised and excited when he agreed, as I was genuinely in love with him and wanted to give life together another chance.

After three months I realized that I was pushing for something he wasn't truly on board with. The agreement felt one-sided, and I also came to understand that I didn't actually want to get married. What my heart truly yearned for was his commitment and loyalty. I didn't want to coerce him into committing if it wasn't genuinely what he wanted. Therefore, I ended things again, this time over a phone conversation. I knew that if I saw him in person, I would be drawn back into the love I still felt for him.

I changed my number and for about six months cut off communication with him until one day something prompted me to reach out again.

We met up for dinner. I was anxious about how seeing him would feel... thankfully, the love I once had for him had turned into self-love, and I knew I had made the right choice. Whew!

After a year in the same city post-breakup, I needed a big change, so I decided to move to Costa Rica... but that's a story for another time.

I believe everything happens for a reason. Looking back, I can appreciate the lessons learned, give thanks to myself for setting those boundaries, and to him for giving me the opportunity to open my heart once more to love. Today, I feel grateful for that relationship. It pushed me to keep working on myself and rediscover the self-love I had been missing. Perhaps if we had established a mutual "relationship/marriage lease" where we both had our needs met, there could have been a chance for the relationship to work out, or maybe not. But now I know to set boundaries and expectations right from the start. At this point in my life, I feel much clearer about what I want in a partnership.

With a marriage lease, having something to look forward to naturally motivates us to become better individuals, not only for ourselves but also for our partners. It's all about mutual growth and support in a relationship. Having clear expectations and boundaries in place can truly make a difference.

I think the concept of a marriage lease for couples who aren't ready to face the pain of divorce is spot on!

Conclusion

Change is certain in life, and I believe the commitment we make to the person beside us should be structured to flex and bend with that change. A marriage lease can be an important step in the journey. As we saw in these pages, this new concept can help us see traditional marriage with new eyes, particularly within the context of relationships formed later in life.

I hold a deep respect for traditional marriage, particularly for young couples starting families. I was in one myself for many years with my young family. My experiences from that time and the decades after the divorce shaped many of the ideas in this book. I hope it will pique the interest of committed couples wanting an unconventional approach to marriage, as well as people who divorced and would do anything not to face the legal and religious systems again. A marriage lease agreement can also easily integrate into a traditional marriage for couples of any age. The habit of regular check-ins and open communication about how needs are being met or unmet can enrich almost every human connection.

I want to encourage you to connect with this new concept with open hearts and open minds, seeing how it can help build strong, resilient, and satisfying partnerships.

Whether you're thinking about it on your own, talking with your loved ones, or joining discussions with others, let's experiment with this new concept and see how it fits into our changing world.

To help you get started here is an example of a fictional marriage lease that illustrates some of the key structural points. I hope you will take this sample and develop it into an agreement that lays out what is most important to you and your partner. Some of the earlier chapters may inspire your conversation. I imagine some very colorful dialogue around the second point on the sample below, "Rights and Responsibilities". Take this and have fun with it!

47

Marriage Lease Agreement

This Marriage Lease Agreement ("Agreement") is entered into by and between [Partner 1 Name], residing at [Address], and [Partner 2 Name], residing at [Address], on this [day month year].

1   The Agreement commences on the aforementioned date and renews automatically for subsequent one-year terms unless modified or terminated by either partner in accordance with the terms of this Agreement.

2   Rights and Responsibilities: a. Both parties shall be responsible for contributing to the emotional well-being and support of each other. b. Both parties shall contribute to the household responsibilities, including but not limited to cooking, cleaning, and financial management. c. Both parties shall maintain open and honest communication and work towards resolving conflicts peacefully.

3   Termination: Either party may terminate this Agreement by providing written notice to the other party at least 30 days prior to the end of the current term.

4   Amendments: Any amendments to this Agreement must be made in writing and signed by both parties.

5   Governing Law: This Agreement shall be governed by the laws of love. (Or State)

In witness whereof, the parties have executed this Agreement as of the date first above written.

[Signature of Partner 1]   [Signature of Partner 2]
[Printed Name of Partner 1]   [Printed Name of Partner 2]

(This is a fictional example for illustrative purposes only)

Made in the USA
Monee, IL
07 July 2026